# the secret to happiness

## PRACTICAL ADVICE FOR FINDING JOY IN EVERY DAY

SOPHIE GOLDING

THE SECRET TO HAPPINESS

An Hachette UK Company
www.hachette.co.uk

Vie Books, an imprint of Summersdale Publishers Ltd
Part of Octopus Publishing Group Limited
Carmelite House
50 Victoria Embankment
LONDON
EC4Y 0DZ
UK

www.summersdale.com

Printed and bound in China

ISBN: 978-1-78783-984-7

Substantial discounts on bulk quantities of Summersdale books are available to corporations, professional associations and other organizations. For details contact general enquiries: telephone: +44 (0) 1243 771107 or email: enquiries@summersdale.com.

To.................

From............

# INTRODUCTION

Could I be happier? Is joy something that everyone can find? Are there things I can do to live a happier life? The answer to all of these questions is yes!

The pursuit of happiness is an age-old quest and, in modern life – which puts so many demands on our time and our resources – it is perhaps harder than ever. But it needn't be impossible. Within these pages you'll find tips on inviting harmony into your life, advice on cultivating a positive mindset, and a raft of beautiful quotes and affirmations to inspire you along the way.

We all have the capacity to live happy and fulfilled lives; simply by picking up this book, you've made a positive step in your journey. Now, take the next step: read on to discover the secret to happiness.

THE SMALL HAPPY
MOMENTS ADD UP.
A LITTLE BIT OF JOY
GOES A LONG WAY.

MELISSA McCARTHY

# Finding
# *your* happy

There is more than one way to enjoy a cup of coffee. There is more than one genre of music in the world. And there is more than one route to happiness! We are all individuals, unique from head to toe – from our thoughts, to our experiences, to our favourite TV shows – which means that your path to joy is also your own. There are innumerable ways for you to find happiness, and this book will help you to explore them.

# LOOK
# WITHIN

When searching for happiness, we tend to look for things that we can add to our lives, thinking the answer lies somewhere beyond ourselves. However, we are often our own biggest obstacle when it comes to joy. Although it's true that our mood is determined by factors beyond our control – such as genetics or circumstance – a large part of happiness starts with us, *within* us. The key to finding more of it is learning to be content with who you are, and where you are right now.

# THERE IS A REASON TO SMILE EVERY DAY

# ONE POSITIVE THOUGHT

What's the first thing you think of when you open your eyes in the morning? For many of us, our thoughts immediately jump to the things we're dreading, or everything we have to get through before our heads hit the pillow at the end of the day. This means that before you've even got out of bed, you're already in a negative headspace.

Next time you wake up, try to have a moment of stillness before getting out of bed. Instead of seeing the day as a long stretch of time filled with chores, recognize it as a gift – still ahead of you, full of possibility and yours to make the very most of. Then, find one positive thing to look forward to. Maybe you will see a friend at work, or it's the day that a new episode of your favourite show is aired. If you can't think of anything, try turning something you feel is negative into a positive (e.g. "I'll feel satisfied when I have submitted my project today."). This sets a positive tone for your day.

"

**WITH THE NEW DAY
COMES NEW STRENGTH
AND NEW THOUGHTS.**

ELEANOR ROOSEVELT

# FIND YOUR TRIBE

Do you have people in your life who encourage your negative thoughts? Do you ever come away from social events feeling drained or down? Our happiness levels are affected by the people we spend time with, so if you're regularly mixing with people who don't bring you joy, you'll probably find it much harder to be positive in your day-to-day life. Try to minimize your time with these people and, instead, surround yourself with those who support you and make you feel great.

# SURROUND YOURSELF WITH SUNSHINE

# Smile!

If you're having a bad day, or you just can't seem to muster any energy, try smiling to yourself. It will probably feel silly and be the last thing you want to do (especially if you're feeling down) but this simple action could boost your mood. Smiling is a trigger for a powerful chemical reaction in your brain – the release of endorphins, your body's natural feel-good hormones. Your body can't tell whether a smile is real or fake, so this is a quick way to give yourself a boost, even on bad days.

# Laugh

From grinning to giggling – did you know that laughter can be a powerful contributor to your health and happiness? Not only does it release endorphins, which make you feel happy, but there are also proven health benefits: it reduces your levels of stress hormones such as cortisol, it lowers your blood pressure and it can even give your immune system a boost. To bring more laughter into your life, you could think back on funny memories and reminisce about them with a friend, sit back and enjoy a funny film or TV show, or watch some stand-up comedy.

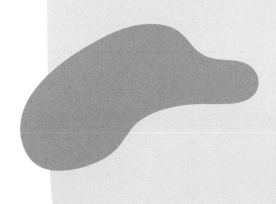

# LAUGHTER IS AN INSTANT VACATION.

MILTON BERLE

# SELF-CARE ISN'T SELFISH

# TIME FOR YOU

When life is busy and you're rushed off your feet, it's hard to make time for yourself – but this is exactly when self-care is most important! Make "me-time" a regular, non-negotiable part of your schedule where you try to focus on just relaxing, and don't set yourself any tasks or expectations. Life is hectic enough, without the added pressure we put on ourselves to remain constantly productive. You'll soon realize that even just a little bit of downtime can boost your mood.

# LOVE YOURSELF

You may well find it easy to list the things that you don't like about yourself – but what about the things you do like? Stand in front of a mirror and look yourself in the eye. Focus on everything that you love about yourself. List physical attributes – your eyes, your curves, your dimples – but don't forget about the things you can't necessarily see on the outside. What do you love about your personality? What are your talents? What makes you unique? By regularly bringing your attention back to the things that you like and value about yourself, you will cultivate deep contentment and a sense of self-worth.

# REMIND YOURSELF THAT YOU ARE WONDERFUL!

# YOU DESERVE HAPPINESS

To find happiness, we must first believe that we deserve it; this might sound obvious, but we can be remarkably harsh on ourselves. The negative self-talk that we subject ourselves to is often much stronger than anything we'd say to a friend, and this harms our self-esteem, making us feel we aren't good enough. Over time, this can really affect our overall happiness and well-being. Instead, be your own cheerleader. Make a conscious effort to tell yourself that happiness is a priority, and it's something that you fully and completely deserve.

# Love your quirks

Be gloriously you! When we feel free enough to be ourselves, happiness usually follows. So, don't apologize for who you are, and resist any urge to make yourself smaller to accommodate others. Embrace all your quirks, your flaws, your interests and the things that make you unique, because these aspects all put together are what make you YOU!

YOU ARE
WORTHY OF
THE LOVE
YOU GIVE
TO OTHERS

# Do what you love

So much of our lives is taken up with the things we have to do – chores, admin, work – so carve out some time to do the things that you love, too. If you have a hobby or passion that keeps getting sidelined, consider how you could prioritize it (schedule it if you have to!). If you're not sure what you love, think about what you used to do when you were young and follow that path. Did you run, dance or paint? Did you love inventing things or baking? Have fun trying out activities and reconnecting with the things that make you happy.

# A MULTITUDE OF SMALL DELIGHTS CONSTITUTES HAPPINESS.

## CHARLES BAUDELAIRE

# TINY PLEASURES

When we think of what makes us happy, we often picture the big events in life, but there is plenty of joy to be found in the everyday too. Take notice of all the good parts of your day – the small things that you might not always appreciate. Maybe the sun was shining, or you had a great cup of coffee, or you shared a laugh with a friend. These little moments of happiness add up, and once you start paying attention you'll soon appreciate how much simple joy can be found in the everyday.

# Gratitude journal

Keeping a gratitude journal is a great way to help us focus on the positive aspects of our lives, and it gets us into the habit of finding joy in the little things. Try keeping a gratitude journal and see how it changes your perspective. You can do this for as little or as long as you want, and your journaling style can be simple or complex depending on what feels natural to you.

All you need to do is record the things that you are grateful for each day. It's up to you whether you write down single words, one line per day, or journal in more detail. There are many different forms your journal could take – you might record your notes in a traditional notebook, type out your thoughts onto your phone, or you could jot some observations onto sticky notes.

Alternatively, there are many beautiful gratitude journals that contain daily prompts to inspire you. When you train yourself to be mindful of all that you have to be grateful for on a daily basis, your outlook will naturally become more positive.

# A daily goal

At the beginning of each day, set yourself one goal. It can be big or small. It could be a practical task you've been putting off, or it could be something that helps you move toward a larger objective. A goal gives your day purpose, and when you complete it, you'll gain a sense of achievement that can feel deeply satisfying. Here are a few examples:

- I will tidy that drawer/shelf/room
- I will be kind to myself all day
- I will get dressed today
- I will give myself at least three compliments throughout the day
- I will move through my day with a positive mindset

# I WILL WALK

# THE PATH

# OF HAPPINESS

# ONE STEP

# AT A TIME

# THE ART OF THE TO-DO LIST

A common reason that we are unhappy is because our stress levels are high – and our stress levels are often high because we are busy. If you're ever feeling overwhelmed, writing a simple to-do list can work wonders for your mental health, giving you peace of mind as well as boosting your productivity! Here's how to create an effective to-do list:

1   Write a master list. This should include every single task – even the tiny things! Keep updating this list as days and weeks go by.

2   Break any big tasks into smaller steps that you can take to complete them. For instance, instead of "Plan holiday", you might write "Research accommodation" and "Book flights".

3   Go through the list and rank each job by importance. You could number items 1–3 by their urgency, or you could colour-code them.

4   Finally, take it one day at a time. Pick a few tasks every day from your master list that you know you will be able to accomplish.

Using this method will enable you to keep track of everything you need to do, as well as encourage you to organize your day more efficiently – and a weight will be lifted off your shoulders.

"

HAPPINESS, NOT IN
ANOTHER PLACE BUT
THIS PLACE, NOT
FOR ANOTHER HOUR
BUT THIS HOUR.

WALT WHITMAN

# Make a mood board

Mood boards aren't just for fashionistas and designers – they can help you to visualize your dreams and focus on your happiness. If you have a particular goal that you're working toward, a mood board of images, clippings and quotes can help to keep you motivated. You could also make a mood board that inspires joy! Keep an eye out for photos, colours, fabrics or poems that make you happy and add them to your board. This is a great project to work on over time – watch it grow and develop, and be reminded of things that uplift you every time you look at it.

# TREAT YOURSELF

To keep your spirits up, indulge in a treat every day. It doesn't have to be extravagant – even just having something small to look forward to will buoy you up and help you get through any difficult parts of the day. Plan to go on a walk or a run in the evening, meet up with a friend for a coffee, have some chocolate biscuits or a bubble bath, or enjoy an evening of quality time with a loved one.

# SEEK

# MAGIC

# EVERY

# DAY

# DO A GOOD DEED

An act of kindness doesn't only help the recipient – it lifts you up too! Keep an eye out for moments in your day when you could help someone else. You could hold open a door, make someone a hot drink or a meal, offer to do a neighbour's shopping for them, smile at a passer-by, let a fellow shopper go before you in a queue, leave a good review for a restaurant or small business, offer to help a friend with a task, or pay your colleague a compliment. You never know the difference just one small act of kindness could make to someone's day, and by showing true generosity of spirit to others you also enhance your own sense of well-being.

# HAPPINESS COMES WHEN YOUR WORK AND WORDS ARE OF BENEFIT TO YOURSELF AND OTHERS.

JACK KORNFIELD

# CELEBRATE THE THINGS THAT MAKE YOU SMILE

# Share your joy

We're often taught as children that it's wrong to boast, and it can be hard to put ourselves into the spotlight when we're not used to it. But we shouldn't be shy about sharing our achievements when things go well. Next time something good happens to you, tell others! The people who love and care about you will want to hear about it – and sharing your happiness with others can even increase it.

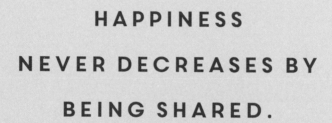

# HAPPINESS

## NEVER DECREASES BY

## BEING SHARED.

BUDDHIST SAYING

# A fresh view

When we fall into a routine, we tend to stop noticing what's around us – but the world is full of new things to see and appreciate every day. For example, even if you're walking a familiar route, make an effort to look up at the world, instead of down at your feet. Be present while you're preparing a meal, noticing the unique shapes of fruits and vegetables or the rich colours and scents of your food. Watch the people who you pass in the street – what could their stories be, and where might they be going? Looking at the world with curiosity and wonder can renew our zest for life.

# FIND THE THINGS THAT MAKE YOU GLOW

# FIND
# YOUR FLOW

Have you ever lost track of time when you've been doing something you enjoy? This is called the "flow state", and it's a kind of energized focus that you experience when you are fully absorbed in what you're doing. According to psychologists, this state, also known as being "in the zone", is where true happiness and fulfilment lies – so take note of and pursue the things that make you feel this way!

# EVERYDAY ADVENTURES

You don't have to wait for the weekend or for a holiday to embark on an adventure – you can have one every day! There's no need to travel to far-flung places or do something that scares you either; a little adventure is something small enough to fit into your day, but interesting enough to breathe some fresh air into your routine.

Perhaps you could wake up in time to see the sunrise, or spend your lunch hour doing a mini scavenger hunt or visiting a café you've never been to before. Your evenings are your oyster too – why not cook with an ingredient you've never used, go stargazing, attend a local music or comedy night or have a mid-week sleepover with a friend?

Life is filled with possibility, so become an everyday explorer and make the most of it. Little glimmers of excitement here and there help to nourish your soul and bring you joy.

# LET GO OF NEGATIVITY

We can't be truly happy until we let go of the things that are keeping us down. If you're holding on to a bad experience, a regret, a grudge or any other negative feeling, try to let it go. Make a deal with yourself that from this moment on, the negativity will remain in the past, and you will move forward and beyond it. If the negative feeling persists, consider speaking to a loved one or a medical professional, to help you move on from it.

IT'S BEEN MY
EXPERIENCE THAT YOU
CAN NEARLY ALWAYS
ENJOY THINGS IF YOU
MAKE UP YOUR MIND
FIRMLY THAT YOU WILL.

LUCY MAUD MONTGOMERY

SMALL

PROGRESS

IS STILL

PROGRESS

# Nothing compares to you

You may be familiar with the phrase "comparison is the thief of joy" – and it's true. It's easy to be disheartened about your own successes because they seem insignificant when compared to someone else's. But comparing ourselves to others stops us from seeing how much we have achieved. We are each on our own journey, so, instead of looking at someone else, refresh your perspective and compare yourself with yourself! Look backward and reflect on how far you've already come!

# Let people in

It's been scientifically proven that social connections make us happier, so, for longer-lasting joy and well-being, make sure to keep up with your friends and family. It's easy to let life drift, seeing the people we value sporadically and only when it happens to be convenient. But we all know the happy glow of coming away from a really good catch-up, or an uplifting evening with the people we love – and that's what makes us happy. So chase that feeling! Be proactive about engaging with your friends and family, and make a conscious effort to invite them into your life.

If your loved-ones live further afield, you could schedule a regular phone call to make sure you catch up, host an online quiz night, or set up a group chat on your social media so it's easy to keep in touch. For friends who live close to you, stay connected by inviting them round, whether it's for dinner, a movie night or just for coffee and a chat.

DO WHAT YOU CAN,
WITH WHAT YOU HAVE,
WHERE YOU ARE.

THEODORE ROOSEVELT

# Volunteer

Giving your time to others makes the world a better place – and it helps to uplift you too! Pick a cause you care about and find opportunities through a specific charity, or follow your interests. You could participate in a beach clean, ask for sponsorship to run a race, donate a small amount of money to a charity effort, help out in a soup kitchen, or volunteer as a telephone befriender. All are worthwhile pursuits and will increase your feelings of self-worth and provide you with a sense of true purpose.

# GIVE COMPLIMENTS

If a colleague has had a haircut and it looks great on them, tell them! If a friend has achieved something, let them know you're proud of them. If you admire someone for a particular trait – perhaps they are confident, funny, or good at giving advice – then say so! Giving compliments not only gives both of you a boost, it helps get you into the habit of noticing the wonderful qualities of the people around you.

# THROW KIND

# WORDS AROUND

# LIKE CONFETTI

# ACCEPT COMPLIMENTS

How did you respond the last time you received a compliment? And how did it make you feel? If your instinct is to brush them off or explain them away, try the following: next time someone gives you a compliment – no matter how small – look the other person in the eye, keep your head up and say thank you. Allow yourself to believe what they are saying, and let their words light you up from the inside. If you feel the urge to belittle yourself, resist it! You deserve to be proud of yourself and your achievements.

If you still find it difficult, think about how it feels when the situation is reversed. You just want the other person to know how highly you think of them, and you'd like to help brighten their day! So, next time someone offers you some kind words, allow yourself to be happy. Why not keep a record of your compliments so that you can look back on them when you're feeling down?

# SAY THANK YOU

Living a life of gratitude is strongly linked to happiness – and all you need to do is to say thank you. Take notice of the times when people help you in your day-to-day life – from the little things, like making you coffee or serving you in a shop, to the big things, like helping out with childcare or solving a problem. You don't just have to thank people; thank the sun for shining, thank the earth for growing your food, and thank your body for everything it does to help you live every day.

A GRATEFUL HEART IS A HAPPY HEART

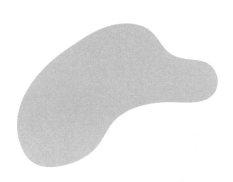

IT'S NEVER TOO
LATE TO TAKE A LEAP
OF FAITH AND SEE WHAT
WILL HAPPEN – AND
TO BE BRAVE IN LIFE.

JANE FONDA

# Try something new

Get yourself out of a rut by trying something new! Pick an activity you've always wanted to try or go for something unexpected just for the fun of it. Join a sports club, dance class or art session, learn a new skill through online tutorials, or ask a friend to introduce you to one of their hobbies to see if you like it too. Stepping out of our comfort zone and trying new things increases our confidence and allows us to take a bigger bite out of life – which, in turn, contributes to our happiness.

# SING

Singing is a wonderful way to increase your happiness. It has a whole host of physical benefits: singing requires that you breathe deeply and hold an upright but relaxed posture – both of which help to calm the body's stress response, decrease muscle tension and increase the levels of oxygen in your blood. Singing also triggers the release of endorphins – the body's "happy hormones" – which provides a feel-good boost. If you join a choir, there are many social benefits too; it's a great way to meet and connect with new people, and singing together has been proven to forge social bonds.

Finally, singing is fun! Whether you want to be part of a huge group or a handful, whether you want to sing pop songs, musical numbers or classical masterpieces, there is something out there for everyone. Singing on your own can be just as joyful too – belting out your favourite ballads in the shower or singing along to the radio in your car will still give you a boost and improve your day.

"

ALL THE HAPPINESS
THERE IS IN THIS WORLD
ARISES FROM WISHING
OTHERS TO BE HAPPY.

GESHE KELSANG GYATSO

# Call someone

Call a friend or family member for a catch-up. Even if you just chat for 5 or 10 minutes, having a brief check-in will brighten up your day or your evening, and help you to stay connected. Why not aim to call one person a week? Studies show that if we're having a bad day, calling a loved one will make us feel happier – so next time you need a boost, pick up the phone.

# LISTEN TO MUSIC

Dopamine is one of the feel-good hormones that regulate our mood, and the more we have, the happier we tend to be. Listening to music is one of the things that triggers the brain to release dopamine, so put your favourite tunes on to help you smile. Whether you like listening to pop music, heavy metal, dramatic film scores or calming mood music, your best-loved tracks will help you feel happier.

# Meditate

For those who experience a lot of stress, finding a sense of calm is an important step toward happiness. If you would like more stillness in your life, try meditation. There are many different forms of meditation, but at the heart of all of them is the idea that your mind and body should be in tune with one another, focusing on the present moment in order to find quietude and peace.

To try meditation, find somewhere where you can sit comfortably for a few minutes, undisturbed, and close your eyes. Become aware of your body and your natural breath. Then, begin to deepen your breath; take a long, slow inhale through your nose, and breathe out slowly through your mouth. Focus on your breath and the way that your body feels. If interfering or distracting thoughts rise up, acknowledge them without judgement, but then let them go. Allow your mind to be still.

Meditation can be a tricky skill to master, especially when our minds are used to racing from thought to thought. But even practising it for just a few minutes in the morning can give you a calmer and happier outlook for the rest of the day.

# Hugs!

For an instant mood boost, have a hug! Hugs not only strengthen social bonds, they encourage the flow of oxytocin, also known as the "cuddle hormone". This hormone is what gives you that warm-and-fuzzy feeling, and as well as helping to soothe your nervous system and lower your blood pressure, it promotes your sense of well-being. To maximize the benefits of oxytocin, stay in the hug for at least twenty seconds.

THERE ARE TWO WAYS
OF SPREADING LIGHT:
TO BE THE CANDLE,
OR THE MIRROR THAT
REFLECTS IT.

EDITH WHARTON

# IF YOU WANT TO SEND A SMILE, SEND A LETTER

# Write a letter

Find some paper, pick up a pen and write a letter to a friend or family member. Letter writing can bring joy in many ways. There's the happiness you get from communicating with others, as well as the satisfaction of having created something special and personal for someone you care about. Writing a letter often enables you to open up to someone in a way that you wouldn't over the phone or via a message – it allows you to be more considered, and the connection that you make with the other person is often more meaningful.

# IF YOU WANT
# TO BE HAPPY,
# BE.

## LEO TOLSTOY

# GO GREEN

Spending time in green open spaces has been scientifically proven to improve your mood, so try having breakfast outside in the garden, spending your lunch hour in a local park, or heading out to fields and forests in your spare time to reap the benefits of Mother Nature.

# GET MOVING

Exercise has a whole host of benefits for our minds and bodies. It can reduce stress and anxiety, increase confidence and self-esteem, boost the production of endorphins, and enhance the brain's sensitivity to serotonin – a hormone that relieves feelings of depression. This all leaves us feeling energized and much happier. Getting our bodies moving improves our overall physical health too, so try going for a jog, playing a sport or doing a workout.

If you're not keen on intense exercise – maybe you're just starting out on your fitness journey, or you're unable to move vigorously – there are plenty of other ways to get active. As long as you increase your heart rate, you will feel the benefits of exercise. Why not walk a slightly longer route than usual to get to your destination, sit on a stability ball rather than a chair or do some push-ups or squats while you watch TV or wait for the kettle to boil? No matter what your lifestyle is, there are plenty of small ways to fit movement into it, and thus plenty of opportunities to boost your mood.

# WILD SWIMMING

Wild swimming is a wonderful combination of exercise and getting out into nature – it's also exhilarating! The health benefits of immersing yourself in cold water include the soothing of aches, a reduction in anxiety, plus a diminished response to stress (if done regularly), as well as providing a boost to your immune system and vitality. The immediate endorphin high from wild swimming also makes you feel positive and happy and ready to take on life's challenges.

# BE AT

# ONE WITH

# NATURE

# TAKE STOCK

Your home is the place you come back to every day to relax, unwind and to be yourself – so it should be somewhere that makes you feel comfortable and happy! Put aside some time to take stock of your home and ask yourself whether it brings you joy, or whether there are things you could do to make it a more uplifting space. If you want to create a cosier feel, consider adding in some soft lighting and a few comfy throws – or, for a more vibrant space, try hanging some colourful prints or getting a few houseplants.

# THE GREATEST HAPPINESS IS TO TRANSFORM ONE'S FEELINGS INTO ACTION.

MADAME DE STAËL

# DECLUTTER

Decluttering is the mindful approach to tidying your home. It's not about throwing everything away – instead, it involves looking at what you own and letting go of the things that aren't fully loved or necessary. The very act of tidying can be therapeutic; making small but confident decisions about what you do and don't need allows you to check in with yourself and your life, and helps you to feel in control. Having a tidy and organized space can also have a hugely positive effect on your mood and your outlook on life.

To declutter, first pick an area of your home. Start small if you need to: pick one room, one cupboard or even just one drawer. Then go through everything in that area. If you love it or use it on a regular basis, keep it. If you don't need it, put it in a pile to either get rid of or to give away. If you find yourself keeping an item "just in case", think hard about whether you will ever realistically need it, or if someone else might benefit from having it instead.

# HAPPINESS COMES FROM WITHIN

# Sort your wardrobe

Most of us add to our wardrobe frequently, but decluttering it? Not so much. It can be hard to let go of clothes – we tell ourselves that there will one day be an occasion to wear them again, or particular garments have sentimental value to us. However, saying goodbye to clothes you no longer need or wear can leave you with a clearer outlook and a more positive headspace. Go through your wardrobe and ask yourself the following for each item: Do I love it? Do I ever wear it? Is it itchy or uncomfortable?

# Happy bedroom

Your bedroom is a sanctuary, and it should be treated as such! It's easy for it to become a catch-all space, housing everything from dirty washing to paperwork, but for a restful night's sleep and a more positive outlook, be mindful about how you treat this room.

Ideally, it should be a place for sleep and relaxation, and not associated with work or any other chores that need doing during the day. Keep it free of clutter and only display knick-knacks and pictures that bring you joy. Open the windows for a period each day to allow fresh air to flow through, and regularly change the bedding to keep it crisp, fresh and inviting. Opt for soft lighting and try to keep it screen-free – this includes TVs, tablets, laptops and phones – as the blue light from these devices can make it difficult to fall asleep.

For extra ambience, why not light some scented candles? Scents such as lavender, camomile and vanilla promote relaxation and restorative sleep.

# Make your bed

Making your bed every morning is a small thing that makes a huge difference. Not only does it make your room look more pleasing and inviting, it sets the tone for the day – and it means that you've accomplished something before you've even left your bedroom. It also reinforces the idea that the little things matter, and helps you to take pride in your life and the things that you do – all of which contribute to a more positive outlook.

# STAY CALM AND POSITIVE

# QUICK CLEAN

A tidy home helps with a positive mindset – and so does a clean one. If your heart sinks at the idea of getting out the sponge and disinfectant, take note: although a deep clean is a good idea every now and again, this isn't the only way to make your home sparkle. Get into the habit of doing a couple of minutes of cleaning at a time. Clear the counter in the kitchen after use, or give the bathroom a quick wipe-down after your shower, for instance. This means your home stays fresh and inviting between bigger cleans.

# LIFE TRULY BEGINS AFTER YOU HAVE PUT YOUR HOUSE IN ORDER.

MARIE KONDO

# GET
# HYGGE

Watching the sun rise, sharing a meal, a good conversation with friends – these are the moments that leave us with an inner glow: a sense of satisfaction, fulfilment and peace. This feeling is known throughout Scandinavia as *hygge*, and it's possibly part of the reason that Denmark is one of the happiest nations on earth.

The word hygge doesn't translate into a single word or phrase in English, but it can be understood as the feeling of finding joy in the simple pleasures of everyday life. And – whether you're snuggled in front of the hearth in winter, or feeling the summer sunshine on your cheeks and the grass between your toes – hygge is a state of being that can be enjoyed all year round.

Here are some ideas to help you invite hygge into your life:

- Invest in a cosy pair of pyjamas and slippers
- Enjoy a candlelit dinner
- Go for a woodland walk
- Take a warm bath
- Go on a picnic
- Curl up with a cup of hot chocolate
- Get lost in a book

cultivate

joy

in your

heart

# BRING THE OUTSIDE IN

Choose some houseplants for your home. Not only do they add colour and life to your living space, but they have health benefits too. Plants are said to have a calming effect, and some even have air-purifying properties due to the amount of oxygen that their leaves produce.

# Grow your own

Growing your own fruit, veg, herbs or flowers is rewarding in many ways. Not only is it good for the earth, but it also allows you to spend time in the fresh air and experience the magic of bringing something to life! Whether you have a big garden, a small courtyard or even a windowsill, it's always possible to be green-fingered. Gardening will enrich your life and is sure to become a source of joy.

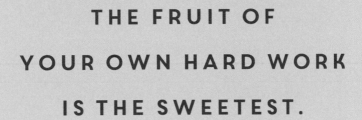

THE FRUIT OF
YOUR OWN HARD WORK
IS THE SWEETEST.

DEEPIKA PADUKONE

# HAPPINESS IS
# A WARM PUPPY.

CHARLES M. SCHULZ

# Animal magic

Spending time with animals lowers our stress levels and increases self-esteem by making us feel needed, so make sure you give your animal companion lots of love. If you don't own a pet, why not offer to look after someone else's? This should be a win-win situation: walking someone's dog, for example, will not only be a favour to the owner, but you'll also get the opportunity to go out into nature and share your experience with a furry friend.

# BEAT MONEY WORRIES

Money worries can be a huge weight on our minds – so get your finances organized to feel a whole lot happier. Create a spreadsheet to keep track of monthly expenditure so that you know exactly how much money is coming in and how much is going out. If you need to save money, shop around for things like energy tariffs and phone bills, to make sure you're getting the best deal, and cancel subscriptions to the things you don't need or use. Though you likely won't solve all your money worries overnight, taking small steps will help you feel more calm and in control.

# HAPPINESS COMES FROM PEACE OF MIND

# EAT WELL

The food we put into our bodies can have a profound effect on our mood, so try to eat food that will help you feel your best! A healthy diet should include at least five portions of fruit or vegetables a day, plenty of water, healthy fats (such as those found in nuts and seeds), protein (which can be found in pulses, eggs and chicken), and iron-rich foods (such as green leafy vegetables). A third of your diet should consist of starchy carbohydrates, such as bread, rice and pasta. These are full of nutrients and one of the body's key sources of energy. To make sure you're getting enough, base each meal around a carbohydrate. Eating three meals a day at regularly spaced intervals will help to maintain your blood sugar levels, which keeps you feeling full as well as helping you to stay alert and awake.

If you don't know where to start, try making a small healthy choice each day – such as having an apple instead of a chocolate bar, or drinking an extra glass of water – as this will go a long way toward making you feel better in both body and mind. It's also an excellent way to start building healthy habits.

# HEALTHY SNACKS

When we're hungry it's usually easiest to reach for the sugary, processed snacks – but this isn't always the best way to be kind to your body! Your blood sugar will spike and then crash leaving you feeling lethargic. Instead, try one of these healthier options:

- Popcorn
- A handful of almonds
- Carrots and hummus
- Blueberries
- Energy balls
- Yoghurt
- Apple slices and peanut butter
- Celery sticks and cream cheese
- Vegetable crisps
- Edamame
- A hard-boiled egg

# ONE CANNOT THINK WELL, LOVE WELL, SLEEP WELL, IF ONE HAS NOT DINED WELL.

VIRGINIA WOOLF

# NOURISH
# TO
# FLOURISH

# Eat joyfully

Keep food from becoming a chore by making it a source of joy! Cook your dream meal from when you were a child, try to recreate the food from your favourite restaurant, or simply cook something you love but don't often eat. If you have recipe books that you never use, pick one and choose a meal to prepare this week. Alternatively, buy an ingredient you've never cooked with before. Who knows – it could become a new favourite! As you sit down to eat the food you have lovingly prepared, be sure to eat slowly and mindfully, savouring every mouthful.

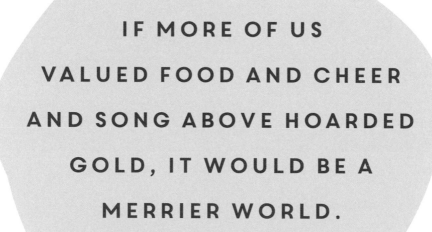

IF MORE OF US
VALUED FOOD AND CHEER
AND SONG ABOVE HOARDED
GOLD, IT WOULD BE A
MERRIER WORLD.

J. R. R. TOLKIEN

# Be drink aware

To keep your body feeling its best, avoid drinking alcohol and caffeine when you can. As well as its negative physical health implications, alcohol has depressant qualities, and caffeine overstimulates us, meaning it commonly causes or exacerbates anxiety. Try herbal or fruit teas and decaffeinated coffee and teas instead, and opt for non-alcoholic beers and wine, or a mocktail – all of which can be just as delicious as the "real thing"!

# STAY HYDRATED

Hydrate to feel great! Employ this simple rule to remember to drink enough water throughout the day – you should be aiming for six to eight glasses, or approximately 2 litres (4 pints). Being dehydrated leads to confusion, irritability, tiredness and feeling light-headed, so to look after your mental health, well-being and overall happiness, make sure you are drinking enough water!

# HAPPY BODY, HAPPY MIND

# UNPLUG

Technology is an incredible tool, but it has its downsides. Whether social media is making you feel down, you find yourself too easily sucked into the mindless scroll, or the effect of blue light is keeping you up at night, a little less screen-time and a little more real-life connection to recharge your own batteries will probably help to keep you feeling happy. Try to set aside some time each week to take a break from your phone, laptop or tablet and enjoy something analogue – whether you read a book, go for a walk or talk to the people you live with.

"

# THE LIVING MOMENT

# IS EVERYTHING.

D. H. LAWRENCE

# SLOW DOWN
# TAKE A BREATH
# TAKE A BREAK

# Go offline

Have digital detox and go offline for the weekend. An extended period of time away from the pressure and noise of technology is always refreshing and puts you back in touch with yourself. Simply let your closest family and friends know that you're signing off, then go out and enjoy life, technology-free! You could plan a camping trip with friends and fill your time with walking, exploring and toasting marshmallows over the campfire, or simply resolve to turn off the Wi-Fi for a weekend and enjoy some undisturbed peace, quiet and tranquillity.

# Be bored

One of the most valuable things you can do for your brain in our always-on world is to allow yourself to be bored. In the quiet moments of the day when brushing our teeth or doing the dishes – in other words, when we're not bombarding ourselves with stimuli – our brains are able to switch gear.

This gear is known as "default mode", a kind of wakeful resting, and it's the human version of autopilot. In this mode, our mind is able to wander and daydream, and as it wanders it makes connections between past experiences and our present. This means that default mode helps us to come up with solutions to problems, to work through issues and to be creative. This mode also helps us to take stock of our lives and get a bearing on our personal narrative, so it allows us to set goals and aspirations for the future too, leaving us feeling calmer, happier and more centred.

So, when you're next confronted with a tedious, routine task, see it not as a drain on your time or a chore, but as an opportunity to let your mind unwind and shift gear.

# Do something silly

We spend so much of our lives being serious – so let off some steam by getting in touch with your inner child and enjoy being silly! Run and jump in puddles, skip down the road, laugh out loud, go on the swings, dangle your legs, play dares, have dessert first, pretend the floor is lava, play party games – the possibilities are endless!

MIX A LITTLE FOOLISHNESS WITH YOUR SERIOUS PLANS; IT IS LOVELY TO BE SILLY AT THE RIGHT MOMENT.

HORACE

# NOTHING COMPARES TO FOOD, FAMILY, FRIENDS AND FUN

# GO FOR A PICNIC

There's something special about eating food outdoors with the breeze in your hair and the grass beneath your feet – so pack up all your favourite treats and a blanket, meet up with friends or family and enjoy a leisurely picnic. Alternatively, just take your food outside! Have your cereal on the front step or eat your lunch in the park instead of the office to experience a little burst of novelty and joy.

# GET A GOOD NIGHT'S SLEEP

We know that exercise and diet contribute to a healthy lifestyle – but did you know that sleep is just as important? If we really want to feel our best and be our happiest selves, a good night's sleep is vital! Everybody is different, but most of us should be aiming for around eight hours of sleep per night. If you have trouble falling and staying asleep try some of the following tips:

- Stick to a bedtime routine. Going to bed and waking up at the same time every day – even on weekends – helps the body to know when it should be winding down and when it should be alert.
- Get the right temperature. Most of us sleep best in a cool room, so try to keep your bedroom between 16 and 18°C (60–64°F).
- Have a hot bath before bed, to help you relax and unwind.
- Use earplugs. If you're a light sleeper or you have noisy neighbours, use earplugs to muffle the sound.
- Keep your room dark, as this helps to signal to your body that it's time to sleep. Invest in thick curtains, or use an eye mask to block out the outside light.

## ACCEPT NO ONE'S DEFINITION OF YOUR LIFE; DEFINE YOURSELF.

### HARVEY FIERSTEIN

# LIVE IN COLOUR

Bring some colour into your life for an instant mood boost. There are a multitude of ways to inject colour into your surroundings; how about painting your walls, choosing fun cushions, rugs or bed linen, using brightly-coloured postcards to decorate your desk or workspace, wearing vibrant clothes or accessorizing your bag with colourful pin badges?

# Be creative

One route to finding happiness and contentment is to let your creativity flow. Give yourself a nice chunk of time – a whole afternoon, if you can – where the only aim is to create something. Write a poem, story or play; paint, draw or sketch; sculpt something from clay; dance to music that speaks to you; write a song; make your own film; try acting; dig out the glue, paper and scissors and get crafting... Whatever you do, express yourself and let your imagination run wild!

# LET YOUR SOUL DANCE

# Love Mondays

Most of us spend a large portion of our lives at work – so it should be a place where we feel happy. Think about your own work situation. Do you leave each day feeling energized and satisfied or unhappy and drained? Does Sunday evening fill you with dread? All jobs will have their ups and downs, but if yours is consistently leaving you feeling down then it might be time to take a new path. You never know what opportunities could be around the corner.

# SURROUND YOURSELF WITH THINGS THAT BRING JOY TO YOUR HEART

# CONNECT WITH YOUR COLLEAGUES

Our work lives improve when we get on with the people we work with, so take some time to get to know your colleagues. Invite someone to have coffee with you in your break or at lunchtime. Strike up conversation in the kitchen, or be the first person to break the ice and offer some friendly comments before a meeting. If you don't usually attend work social gatherings, give one a go. Even if you don't make friends for life, being on good terms with your colleagues can help brighten both your work environment and your outlook.

# "

DOING WHAT YOU
LOVE IS FREEDOM.
LOVING WHAT YOU
DO IS HAPPINESS.

LANA DEL REY

# HAPPINESS IS BY CHOICE, NOT CHANCE

# TIDY UP

They say a tidy desk equates to a tidy mind
– and it's true. Keeping your workspace
neat and organized makes it more inviting,
and it's a simple way to help you feel calm
and ready to take on the day. Declutter
any drawers, invest in a desk tidy to keep
stationery and small items looking orderly
(or make your own if you're feeling creative!)
and make sure the only papers in your
in-tray are the ones that you need.

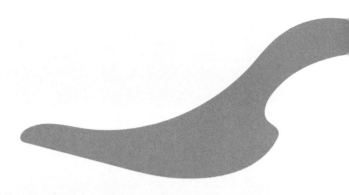

# THE MERE SENSE
# OF LIVING
# IS JOY ENOUGH.

### EMILY DICKINSON

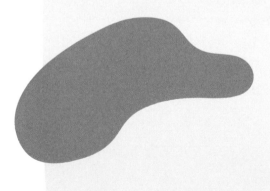

# Take a break

When you're working hard, make sure you remember to take breaks so that you can give your mind and body a rest. It's also important to take regular holiday – because everyone needs time away from the busy routine of life to help them de-stress and recharge. Taking a break has been proven to make us healthier and happier, as well as more productive in the workplace, so there's absolutely no reason to feel guilty about taking some time off!

# STRETCH

If you're sitting down all day, it's important to stretch every now and again, even for just 30 seconds at a time. Not only does this help reduce fatigue and improve circulation, it can do wonders for your mind too, making you feel happier and refreshed. Here are a few stretches you could try:

- Shoulder stretch: Raise your arms above your head, lock your fingers together and turn your palms so they're facing upward. Try to stretch your hands up while keeping your shoulders down. Hold this for a few breaths before bringing your hands down again.
- Chest stretch: Stand up with your feet hip-width apart and look straight ahead. Clasp your hands behind you and then lift them as high as you can. This stretch is particularly good if you spend a lot of time at a computer or desk as it counteracts the effects of hunching over a keyboard.
- Hamstring stretch: Stand with your feet hip-width apart. Bend forward from the hips as far as you can go, keeping your neck and shoulders relaxed. Wrap your hands around the backs of your legs and hold the stretch for 30 seconds. Bend your knees, hold your stomach in and roll up slowly.

# Avoid second-hand stress

When we're surrounded by people who are stressed, it's easy to subconsciously pick up on those feelings and take them on ourselves. If you have people around you who have this effect on your mood – whether it's at home, in your friendship circle or at work – here are a few things to try. Offer some positive advice if someone is focusing on their stress or problems. Alternatively, take yourself out of the situation, whether that's by steering the conversation to more positive ground, or by pausing (or ending) your exchange.

THERE ARE ALWAYS
FLOWERS FOR THOSE WHO
WANT TO SEE THEM.

HENRI MATISSE

# The joy of "no"

The word "no" has a lot of negative connotations, but it can be one of the most positive and freeing words in your vocabulary. We often have the best intentions when we say "yes" to extra tasks or invitations, but more often than not these additional burdens on our time actually end up causing more harm than good. Every "yes" we don't really mean can invite resentment, poor quality work, stress and exhaustion, and can set us up for failure. By saying "no" to things that we don't have time for, or know we won't enjoy, we make room for healthy and fulfilling relationships, for "me time", and for the headspace to actually get our lives in order.

Next time you're asked to do something and you're wondering whether to accept, consider these questions: Do you want to do it? What impact will it have on you? Will you have to make changes to your plans in order to do it? Are the benefits of doing this task worth your time? The prospect of saying "no" can seem daunting at first, especially if we're not used to saying it. However, with practice it becomes easier, and can become your key to a happy and well-balanced life.

# YOU CAN DO ANYTHING, BUT NOT EVERYTHING

# HAPPINESS IS NOT A GOAL; IT IS A BY-PRODUCT OF A LIFE WELL LIVED.

ELEANOR ROOSEVELT

# THE JOY OF "YES"

For peace of mind and for our well-being, it's important to prioritize, and to be able to say "no". However, we also need to have the courage to say "yes"! Saying "yes" can mean pushing yourself out of your comfort zone and doing the new thing that you've always wanted to try, whether that's belly dancing, skydiving or birdwatching. Saying "yes" can lead to adventure – it brings about the spontaneous things that you never planned for but that often end up being some of your favourite memories.

Saying "yes" can also mean choosing a positive mindset. When faced with a difficult task or something you've never done, it's easy to listen to negative self-talk and assume that you can't do it, or that it's too hard. But when you choose positivity, you're choosing to say "yes" – you're choosing the belief that you can and you will. If something feels right to you, or the challenge of it excites you, try to find the inner-confidence to say "yes" to it!

# FIND A
# PURPOSE

One of the keys to happiness is to have a sense of purpose in your life; one of the common ways people find this is through their line of work. For instance, you might feel a calling to help others by being a doctor or teacher, or follow a passion by training to become a chef or a designer. However, your purpose doesn't have to take up the most time in your life – in fact, anything can be your purpose, as long as it leaves you feeling fulfilled. Perhaps you have a charity you volunteer with in your spare time or a project that you are working on, or maybe you have a family that you orientate yourself around. A purpose can be anything that gives you a feeling of direction and meaning. Your purpose doesn't have to remain the same throughout your life either, because what brings you joy at 25 is often different to what fulfils you at 65 – it can grow and change as you do.

# FOCUS ON THE PRESENT MOMENT

We spend a lot of our lives dwelling on the past and planning for the future, but how much time do you spend living in the present? Take a few minutes each day to focus on where you are right now. Consider this physically (what can you feel, see and hear?) and more generally (what are your emotions, what is your life like today, and what matters to you right now?). When you connect with yourself and your life in the present moment, making sure that you experience today in all its fullness, a happier mindset tends to follow.

The present
moment is all
we ever have —
so enjoy it!

# HOLD ON TO HOPE

Allow yourself to be optimistic! It might seem like the smart decision to be a pessimist, if you expect the worst, you'll be prepared when it happens – but scientists have linked optimism with longer life expectancy, mental resilience and greater happiness. So, hold on to hope – it's the light that keeps us going when things get tough, and with a mind that's focused on the positive rather than the negative we will see the world in a more positive light.

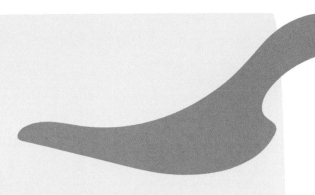

# HAPPINESS DEPENDS

# UPON OURSELVES.

## ARISTOTLE

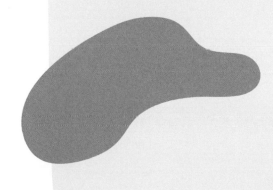

# Use affirmations

An affirmation is a word or short phrase that you can say to help centre and focus yourself. Affirmations can be used for all manner of situations: to help you control anger, motivate you, boost your self-confidence or, in this case, inspire a positive outlook. When you need a boost, you can write down your affirmation, recite it to yourself or, best of all, say it out loud while looking in the mirror. Look yourself in the eye, hold your head up, release the tension from your shoulders and state your affirmation to your reflection with as much confidence and assurance as you can.

The key to affirmations is focusing on the positive outcome that you want rather than the negative possibility that you wish to avoid. Write your own, specific to your circumstances, or try any of the following phrases to set an intention for your day:

- Today is a good day
- I inhale positivity and exhale negativity
- I am right where I need to be
- I deserve happiness
- I am enough

# LET YOUR HAPPINESS LIGHT YOU UP FROM THE INSIDE

# Happiness is a journey

If you're looking to bring more happiness into your life, remember that it's a feeling, not a permanent state of being. Like all other emotions, it will ebb and flow, and some days will inevitably be happier than others. So, instead of thinking of happiness as the destination, see it as a journey; the best thing you can do is to understand yourself and aim to cultivate a happy lifestyle full of the things that reduce your stress and increase your joy.

# FINAL THOUGHTS

There is no single route to happiness – everybody will go on their own path to find their own brand of joy. We are all unique individuals with different lives; some may find that a good work-life balance is what reduces their stress and makes them happy, while another person might realize that it's being kinder to themselves and giving themselves permission to be happy. Hopefully this book will have shone a light on some of the paths you could take, and will help you to discover your own direction.

Although we might think that there is a secret formula for happiness, it's not really a secret at all. Happiness is partly about engaging with the world around us and appreciating the wonderful things life has to offer, but, more than that, it's about understanding and connecting with yourself – so the secret to finding happiness... is you!

If you're interested in finding out more about our books, find us on Facebook at **Summersdale Publishers** and follow us on Twitter at **@Summersdale**.

**www.summersdale.com**